So . . . Help Me, Lord

Prayers of inspiration which celebrate the pleasures, frustrations, and unique solitude of being a man.

Spanning the whole gamut of emotions from the male point of view, here are words of compassion for a wife's umpteenth attempt to lose weight and angry thoughts over income tax, the second-honeymoon feelings of a weekend away from the children, the appreciations of the special joy and anguish of fatherhood.

Here, too, are a man's quiet reflections on the beauty of nature, and his impatience with preachers, hippies, the business world, a teen-ager's guitar — all ending on an optimistic note and a resolve with the Lord's help to understand and act better in the future.

So . . . Help Me, Lord

Alton H. Wilson

DOUBLEDAY & COMPANY, INC.
GARDEN CITY, NEW YORK
1974

Library of Congress Cataloging in Publication Data

Wilson, Alton H
    So . . . help me, Lord.

    Poems.
    I. Title.
PS3573.I45675S6   811'.5'4
ISBN 0-385-02967-5
Library of Congress Catalog Card Number 73–20537

To the three in my life who were both the inspiration for and the subjects of this book:

Janet—My Wife
Martha—Daughter #1
Melissa—Daughter #2

Lord,
I sit here on a fallen log
In my shaded mountain sanctuary
And watch the steeply descending forest
Stretch to flower-carpeted meadows below.
The wild geraniums in numberless profusion
Are like a thousand Milky Ways under
My feet.
While a ruby-throated hummingbird
Darts around my red head,
Thinking she has found a feeder,
The sun sneaks its rays
Through a maze of trees, limbs, and leaves
To find a spot in the meadow
To bless by its warming presence.
An orange-and-brown-winged butterfly
Caresses one flower, then another
And I remember it was once a caterpillar.
A squirrel fusses in a distant tree
At enemies known or unknown
As he issues a "no trespass" warning.
It is at times like this
I recall You are Lord
Of all things great and small.
The butterfly, the squirrel, the hummingbird,
The fallen tree, the sun's ray, the wild geranium.
All these are Your creation
And receive Your blessings.
I am amazed, Lord,
At the pains You have taken
To make the world so beautiful.

So . . . help me, Lord,
        To remember that if You love all these
        Small things,
        How much You love me.

Lord,
I once thought Your plan for me
Was success.
I tried so hard to help You,
Only to find failure.
But in the process
I found You.
Thank You, Lord,
That it is not the end You have in mind at the moment,
But the process.
This is Your training ground for me.
It is *now* You walk with me,
In the midst of the chaos of life,
Not in the sweet by and by.
In this school of obedience
Your grace *is* sufficient.
Were I as successful as I hoped,
I would not need your grace.
Thank You, Lord,
For every fulfilling failure.
It isn't fatal . . .
It only hurts that way.

So . . . help me, Lord,
To learn in failure.

Lord,
I would walk like Enoch.
I wonder . . .
Was he surprised that day
When he went for that walk
and walked on Home with You?

How I love my solitary walks, Lord.
Our communion is somehow closer then.
My concern, Lord, is not my physical walk
But my daily spiritual walk with You.
Enoch must have had a wonderful daily walk
To be "taken" as he was.
Was it hard for him to walk as it is for me?
Some days we walk in unbroken fellowship,
And some days we seem to take altogether different paths.
Teach me, Lord,
To "walk in the spirit"
Rather than by impulse.
On impulse, Peter walked
On the water to You;
But on dry land, he walked afar.
I, too, Lord,
In my high moments
Walk so boldly.
But in the darkness,
When there is no feeling,
When it takes determined faith
I falter.
Oh, Lord,
I do not long to walk on water . . .
I want to be a steadfast dry-land walker.

So . . . help me, Lord,
        To walk by faith "in the spirit."

Lord,
I know how David felt
When he wanted to flee to the mountains.
I, too, long to flee.
Not just for myself,
But for my beautiful, innocent children.
The world so threatens us, Lord.
It seeps in like thick fog.
It creeps in like a roach.
It slithers in like a snake.
And this raging within me is because
I stand helpless against it.
I did not create the mobs,
The drugs, the wars, the poverty, the pornography.
Nor can I protect my loved ones against it.
The foundations are being destroyed, Lord,
And I cry, I moan, I pray.
I know it would do no good to flee.
For there is no escape . . . not even in the mountains.
The world is there, too.
Thank You, Lord,
For praying for me once
That I would be kept from evil in the world.
I remember You said You were sending me *into the world*
Even as Your Father sent You.

So . . . help me, Lord,
            To occupy joyfully in this world
            Until You take me to the next.

Lord,
Do most parents begrudgingly relinquish their young
To the encroaching years?
I remember her, Lord,
As the tiniest, most delicate, porcelain-faced
Red-haired bundle of love.
She was my first-born.
How warm and tender have been our years.
Her call of "papa" never fails to touch me.
But, Lord, she is becoming a young woman,
And, I trust, a lady.
I am losing my little girl, Lord.
I shall miss the child,
Even as I welcome the youth.
Her body is becoming mature,
And I watch, a little sadly.
Not that I would want it otherwise,
But I shall miss the little girl.
And I do so dread the grown-up world
That will become hers.
I know I cannot keep her, Lord,
But I do ask You to comfort the void in my heart
As I watch the child become "grown-up."

So . . . help me, Lord,
        To love the youth as much as the child.

Lord,
As she sang "I wish I had given Him more"
I too wished that I had not only given You more . . .
But all.
Most of the time I thought I had,
And I tried.
But as I look in retrospect,
I see I reserved so much.
Thank You, Lord,
That You knew I wanted to give all,
And You accepted my "want to"
Even when my performance did not match my desire.
Paul felt the same way, Lord,
For he said he could not do those things he longed to do,
Nor help doing the things he did not want to do.
So I am not alone.
Now I must think, not of the past,
But of the here and now.
This moment, Lord, I give to You.
I shall not moan or weep over the past,
Nor dream of the future,
But give myself to You . . . here . . . now,
With no promises.
Accept my love gift, Lord.
Myself is all I can give.

So . . . help me, Lord,
        To freely and fully give just now.

Lord,
Your grace *is* sufficient.
Not "will be"
For it cannot be stored up for future use,
But . . . *is* . . . *here* . . . *now.*
It is never too soon, or too late,
But timed to the tick of the clock
And the beat of my needy heart.
The supply is limitless, inexhaustible,
And present tense.
Knowing You, Lord, has not given me
An immunity to life's problems,
To sin, or to my "self."
I have no built-in escape hatch
To deliver me when things get hot . . . when it's rough.
Your way is far better, Lord, though harder,
And my flesh rebels against the troubles,
The pain, the agonies of life
And longs for a miracle
That will bring ease, sweetness and ecstasy.
It would be so much quicker, and painless . . . and fruitless.
Thank You, Lord,
That You do not give automatic, instantaneous deliverance,
But You *do* give grace,
And it *is* sufficient.
I need only remember it is so
And lean heavily on that sufficiency.

So . . . help me, Lord,
  Not so much to want a miracle
  As to prove in my own life that
  Your grace *is* sufficient.

Lord,
It seemed such a "folksy" lesson at the time.
Too "homespun" to be very valuable.
How wrong I was.
The years have proved that lesson to be 24-karat gold.

She pruned the rosebushes and spoke softly,
Simply saying she did it to bring forth beautiful roses,
And that without the cutting away
The roses would not be beautiful or fragrant.
She reminded me that You would do that to me, Lord,
If I were to be "fruit bearing" and fragrant.
She was right.
The "cutting" has been painful always,
But oh, so necessary.
I thank You, Lord,
That You have been unmerciful in Your pruning,
And have let my cries go unheeded.
Not because You are unmerciful
But You knew only the cutting and pruning
Could produce the beauty of Yourself in me.
Forgive the times I have asked You to let up,
Or stop.
I do want the beauty of Jesus to be seen in me.
I do want to be a sweet-smelling savor of Your grace.

So . . . help me, Lord,
        To remember the rosebushes.

Lord,
Is it so different with me?
Big sins I seem to overcome,
But the little foxes still spoil my vine.
I guard so diligently
The gross sins.
But the trivial things,
The petty, insignificant sins knock me for a loop.
They sneak up on me
And overwhelm me.
To my consternation I find myself
Belittling, condemning,
Unforgiving, jealous,
Sensitive.
Oh, Lord,
How much of the bigness in us do we sacrifice
At the shrine of "the little foxes,"
And in so doing
Become less like Thee.

So . . . help me, Lord,
        To guard . . . and overcome "the little foxes."

Lord,
I sometimes feel as if we are strangers
Though we have walked together for years.
Was this what You had in mind
The day You asked Philip
"Yet hast thou not known me"?

The language I know.
I can speak it fluently.
The prayers I know.
I can pray them piously.
About You, I know.
But *You,* Lord,
I know *You* so little.
Otherwise there would be no miff,
No tearing heart
When I am rebuffed;
No pang of self-pity,
No, nor a streak of remorse.
There would be quietness and rest.
Complete confidence . . . brokenness . . . tenderness.
And love for others.
Much fruit, borne naturally.
Teach me, Lord, the intimacy
Of obedience and discipleship.

So . . . help me, Lord,
        Not to know *about* You . . .
        But to *know* You.

Lord,
The melody is there,
But today . . . well, today
I just don't *feel* like singing it!
Or humming,
Or even hearing it.
Today, Lord,
Let me enjoy my burdens.
For a while I want to
Nurse my grudges
    Pamper my peeves and
       Revel in my slough of despond.

There are times, Lord,
When life is not a song.
It is not a butterfly wing,
Or early morning mist on the mountains.
And all the saccharine-sweet words,
Or happy thoughts, or pretty prayers
Don't set things right.
Everyday is *not* excitement.
Most days are ordinary, plodding days.
Thank You, Lord,
That when I don't feel like a song
I don't have to sing.
I can be *me* with *You.*
You will not scold, or condemn—or impose.
But You ARE there,
Waiting, and hurting with me.
The way I feel is transitory.
Tomorrow I *may* sing.
Whether I sing or scowl
You do not change.

Nor does your love for me.
And thus I am restored.

So . . . help me, Lord,
    In song . . . or in sorrow.

Lord,
It was one of those rare times
When you unexpectedly overhear a gem.
She was only two years old.
It was summertime, and she was in the back yard
With all her dolls lined up in a row
Playing church.
Reverently she took one doll,
Probably her first convert,
And began a baptismal service.
With all the solemnity the occasion deserved, she said
"I baptize you in the name of the Father,
And of the Son . . .
And in the hole you go . . ."

Lord, You must have broken up as we did.
It was too much.
I felt giddy, exhilarated with joy,
For I had heard the beauty and innocence and love
Of a child in one brief sentence.
I was almost overcome with awe, Lord,
For it was a hallowed moment.
I think You must have loved it, too.

She beautifully misinterpreted,
And I wonder, Lord,
How often I have done the same when You have spoken?
It wouldn't be so bad if my misinterpretations
Were as delightful as hers,
But mine lead to problems and heartache.
I hear what You say,
But it gets garbled in the translation.

So . . . help me, Lord,
        To listen, and live as You have spoken.

Lord,
There are times I feel as alone as Elijah,
And with far less reason.
At other times, I just want to pout . . . like Jonah,
Not really knowing why.
Sometimes Jeremiah is my cup of tea
And I want to weep.
These times are needed, Lord,
So that the times of refreshing and joy
Become more precious.

Life is not a bowl of cherries.
It is more "nitty-gritty" than ecstasy.
And that's great, Lord,
For in the "nitty-gritty" I find
You meet my need.
Not that I don't need You
When my days are happy . . .
I just don't feel my need as much then.
Thank You, Lord,
That when I feel like Elijah
There's a brook Cherith.
When I feel like Jonah
There's a gourd vine.
When I feel like Jeremiah
You let me weep, and remind me that
"Weeping may endure for a night,
But *joy* cometh in the morning."

So . . . help me, Lord,
        When I feel alone, or pout, or weep.

Lord,
The house has been so silent.
The giggles and screams,
The laughter and running,
The crying and fussing . . . it's gone.
The girls are at Grandma's,
And our little house is suddenly big.
How wonderful to have a grandma and grandpa
Especially when they live in the mountains
And have squirrels who eat from their hands.
I know the girls are beside themselves, Lord,
But we do miss them.
The dog especially misses them.
Their absence is a keen reminder
Of the precious gifts they are.
Thank You, Lord,
For the joy and responsibility of being a parent.
Never let the burden of the responsibility
Dim the joy of the trust they are to me.

I commit them to You, Lord,
And covenant with You that I will seek,
On this end of the line,
To be to my children as You are to me.
And I ask You to overshadow them with Your presence.
Lead them in a plain path.
Protect them, as I would were I with them.
Love them, as I do,
And keep them innocent as children,
Pure as young people,
And holy as adults.

So . . . help me, Lord . . .
        And my precious children.

Lord,
I've looked for a miracle so long.
It hasn't come.
Nothing has changed.
I face the same things, the same people,
The same needs.
I have prayed so earnestly,
I have wept so many tears.
I just did not realize
You were at work all the time.
The thing most needed was a change . . . in me.
You have been doing that, Lord.
I was too blind to see
There was no other way I could have been changed.
The circumstances . . . the people . . . the problems . . . the needs.
All were designed by You, Lord,
And inexorably, though slowly,
They have fulfilled their purpose.
You did not change my world
But You changed me in the midst of my world.
And because of that world.

So . . . help me, Lord,
        to keep being changed into Your image.

Lord,
She finally fell asleep just now
Holding firmly to my hand.
Her fever has raged high all day,
And I have felt utterly helpless.
Is there anything that so moves a father
As his sick child?
Especially when she is a beautiful little redhead
So full of love, tenderness, and unselfishness.
Lord, You had mercy on Jairus
When his little girl was sick.
Be as gracious to me.
I now can know the heart of Jairus
More than ever before.
He hurt because his child hurt,
And his heart grieved when he thought she was gone.
But Jairus had great faith,
And I would have faith like him, Lord.
I can even understand Your Father heart more now
When I remember You saw Your Son suffer
And had to forsake him.
What a heart-wrenching moment for You, Lord.
So, because I know You understand,
I lift my daughter to You.
Thank You, Lord,
For touching and healing her body.

So . . . help me, Lord,
        By helping my daughter.

Lord,
I thank You for my "in-laws."
How wonderful it has been to grow in love and respect
For them, and see it returned so warmly.
It is no small thing to give your daughter to an outsider.
It is bigger still to make him an "insider."
They have done that, Lord,
And I love them for it.
Their stalwart faithfulness to You
Has made me want to be more faithful.
Their strength has given me strength,
And their unselfishness has taught me much
About You.
I shall always be grateful for the memories
Of shared vacations and holidays,
Shared joys and sorrows.
And Lord, the many times in their mountain home
That have almost saved my life.
They have made such wonderful memories
For my children . . . their grandchildren.
I thank You, Lord, for them.
And for their daughter.

So . . . help me, Lord,
        To remember them when some young man becomes my
        son-in-law.

Lord,
Here under the azure sky,
With fleecy white clouds exploring the heavens
While the warm bright sun bathes the earth,
And the velvety green pines enmesh the singing winds,
I stand in awe on my mountain top
And can only think how wonderful is my God.
My heart nearly bursts
With the joy of living,
And more with knowing I am Thine.
My lips can only praise
The wonder of the Creator
As I stand amazed with His creation.
It does not even sound cheap
To simply and deeply say,
"I love You, Lord."
Oh, my Lord,
These hallowed moments of heart worship
Are far too few.
Moments when the heart and soul
And all that is within me
Cries "holy, holy, holy."

So . . . help me, Lord,
      To worship and adore Thee.

Lord,
What a beautiful morning.
The air is crisp, and as I look below
From these majestic heights,
I see the fog rolling in layers below
Like great puffs of smoke from a thousand chimneys,
Whitened by the bright early sunshine.
The pine and spruce are shimmering
In crystalline beauty,
Like lighted Christmas trees
As the sun makes a diamond of each raindrop
Still clinging to the leaves
After the night rain.
There goes a hummingbird
Piercing every honey-throated foxglove.
I hear a quarreling squirrel in the distance
As a black bird flys by with his raucous "caw caw."
The rain came during the night
And the whole earth is fresh.
The pines are fragrant,
And here and there is a patch of ice
Left from the hail.
Not three feet away a small yellow bird
Perches on a limb,
While off to the right sits a junco.
Oh Lord, the earth is Thy footstool,
And You have made it wondrously beautiful.
Thank You, Lord,
For this time alone this morning
In fellowship with my Creator and His Creation.

So . . . help me, Lord,
        To rejoice always in the beauty of the earth.

Lord,
In her childish prayer she spoke
Such profound wisdom
When she prayed, "Lord, thank
You, for me."
At first I thought it a
Presumptuous prayer,
Until I remembered that You told
Us to give thanks in everything.
I thought it was a sign of
Humility to downgrade myself to You, Lord.
I felt self-effacement was the
Proper approach You wanted.

How wrong I was, Lord.
Your Word says I am redeemed—
Bought back—
By the precious blood of Christ.
This is the deepest truth I have
Ever found, Lord,
And the most unfathomable.
But if You loved me that much
I must be important to You.
And to think I have never thanked
You before for me.
Lord, I do thank You now for me.
I am important to You.
In Your over-all plan of things
I somehow am the object of Your love.
Forgive me for taking myself
As nothing,
When in Your sight I am so loved

As to have been purchased with
The precious blood of Christ.

So . . . help me, Lord,
To take none of Your gifts lightly.
Even me.

Lord,
I want my children to remember
Joy . . . love . . . peace . . . happiness . . .
When they remember me.
I do so want to instill in them
The joy of living,
A lack of fear,
A dauntless faith,
A courageous determination,
An eternal optimism.
But, Lord,
I so often do the opposite.
I fear . . . and see it in them.
I know there is little hope
For my children to grow up in a sane world,
Or even grow up.
I see a world gone mad.
I feel the swift onrush of Satan.
Yet I know the real test for me
Will be in maintaining a calm,
Fearless faith . . . and imparting this to them.
I do so want to teach them that life must be buoyant
Even in the sea of despair that engulfs us.
Lord,
I am not equal to the task,
But my eyes are on Thee.

So . . . help me, Lord,
          To be bright in the darkness.

Lord,
It is getting gloriously dark.
You told us it would be this way
Before Your return.
But that does not lessen my dread of the night.
Keep me from gloom and despair
And help me rejoice as things get worse.
I pray, Lord,
That as the powers of darkness gain control
I shall be bold as Daniel,
Refusing to bow my knee save to Thee.
May I count it joy,
As did the disciples,
To suffer for Your sake.
I am no prophet, Lord,
But it does not take a prophet
To see that judgment is coming.
I do not embrace it,
Nor do I want to be a martyr,
But, Lord, keep me from fear of it.
I know You have not forgotten Your children.
You will provide the needed grace
In the trying hour.
As You walked in the fiery furnace
With the Hebrew children,
So You will walk with all Your children
In the hour of trial.
Lord, strengthen me for the days ahead,
That I might impart optimism and faith
To my children, family and friends.
I cannot say I do not fear,
I only look to You,
Knowing that like Shadrach, Meshach, and Abednego,
We can come through the fire unsinged.

So . . . help me, Lord,
For it is getting gloriously dark.

Lord,
I'm grateful You have not asked me to forsake my humanity.
I enjoy being human.
I revel in its relationships,
Its joys, its sorrows.
I love the smell of the earth after a spring shower,
The pungent odor of a sweating horse.
I thrill at the sight of a verdant valley,
A majestic snow-capped peak,
Or the barren ugliness of volcanic ash.
I love a warm human touch,
Or my dog's cold nose.
I could not respond to these except for being human.
Yet, my humanity wearies me, dulls me,
And drags me irresistibly downward.
I have to live in my own skin,
Suffer my own defeats,
Exult in my own triumphs.
But . . . if that were all
It would not be enough.
Thank You, Lord,
That You have not left us alone in our humanity
To go it by ourselves.
Your Son was clothed in flesh
And thus can understand my humanity.
Because You care, Your Holy Spirit
Indwells this humanity,
Enabling, strengthening, comforting me
In my weakness.

So . . . help me, Lord,
        To yield to Your enabling
        As long as I am in this robe of flesh.

Lord,
Couldn't we just skip the forties?
It's not that I am opposed to getting old,
For age is supposed to reward me
With wisdom and tranquillity.
But the forty-ish years have been so hard.
Life seems to be out of kilter.
The dreams are still future
And the past so void
Of all I had hoped to accomplish.
I suddenly find more of my life
Is behind me than before me,
Without much guarantee that I will
Perform much better in the latter years
Than in the former.
Thank You, Lord,
For the years that go so quickly.
They have been good and friendly,
And have given me more than I deserve.
I guess, Lord, that being in the forties
Is just a rude awakening
To the brevity of life.
I wish I had done better.

So . . . help me, Lord,
    To realize the remaining years will go even more quickly,
    And I must be about my Master's business now.

Lord,
I wish I were a Mr. Fix-it,
But I'm not.
I can't plumb a bathroom,
I can't even plug a leaky
Faucet.
I can't build a house,
Or add on a room,
Or a fireplace, or a patio.
I can't repair a car,
Or even change the oil.
You know how many times I have wished
I could do these things.
If I am not careful, Lord,
I get completely frustrated about it.
Until I read from Your Word
That You created me
And fashioned me,
So that I am physically,
Mentally, emotionally, and in every other way
Your creation.
Out of all the world
You gave me my parents,
My physical heritage,
Past and present,
My emotions, my desires, my abilities.
And You gave me my inabilities
To show me not only my needs,
But Your supply of grace.
So I thank You
For choosing my path,
And the manner in which I walk it.

So . . . help me, Lord,
      To enjoy what You have made me,
            Without envy for what You have made others.

Lord,
I heard the cock crow
In the early morning hours,
And I too wept.
For I knew,
As surely as Peter,
That I had denied You.
Oh, not openly, as he did . . .
I'm more the cowardly type.
Mine was more subtle and smooth.
I'm a little more sophisticated, Lord,
And I have learned how to deny respectably.
But denial it was, and is,
And my heart breaks
For I have more than Peter.
I have the finished testimony of Thy Word,
And the lives of Peter . . . and others
Who have lived saintly lives.
Still I fall . . . and deny . . . and weep.
Thank You, Lord,
For the refreshing power of weeping.
I do love You, Lord!
Three times, like Peter, I can affirm it so.
I am also confident that what You have started
You will bring to maturity,
So that I too may become like the
Post-pentecost Peter.

So . . . help me, Lord,
        To at least weep when I deny.

Lord,
Your timing is always right.
Never too soon . . . never too late.
The testing of Your children is especially timed.
Jonah was in the whale three days,
And came out a changed man.
Daniel had to spend an entire night
With a den full of lions . . . and one angel.
When he got out, an entire nation
Knew You were God of Gods.
The Hebrew children spent time in a fiery trial . . .
Much hotter than any I have known,
Released just on time with their Companion.
Job sat in silence for a week,
Too stunned to speak.
Deliverance was long in coming, or so Job thought,
But it was just at the right time.
And Jesus.
After the cross and the tomb,
He, too, was freed in the resurrection.
Thank You, Lord,
That You know how much Your Children can stand.
You never apply more pressure than we need,
Nor more than we can take.
You know, too, how long we can take it,
And You give relief and release
When one more second's testing would be our undoing.

So . . . help me, Lord,
    To endure, as "seeing Him . . ."

Lord,
"Tis so sweet to trust . . ."
Believing is something else.
I often have to ask You to help mine unbelief.
Through the problems and pain,
The fears and circumstances,
And often through the tears,
I find belief elusive, even impossible.
How sweet then, to trust.
Though I at times cannot believe,
I can always trust.
I can trust because
I can take You at Your Word,
And rest upon Your promises.
I can trust because
You have been faithful in the past,
And You are eternally unchangeable.
"There is no shadow of turning with Thee."
You are trustworthy, dependable.
I can trust because
You have gone this way before me
And You *know* the way I shall take . . .
The end from the beginning . . .
The false from the reality
So that You can guide me in a plain path.
You have already been through it all
And promised You will give me
Only what I can bear.
I can trust because
You are good,
Allowing only that which is best for me.

So . . . help me, Lord,
     To trust when I cannot believe.

Lord,
I guess it just boils down to envy.
When I think of the impetuosity of the Peter
Who could walk on the water,
Or cut off an ear with the sword . . .
And deny his Lord . . . and weep.
I long to walk on water
But I sink.
I long to swath a course by the sword,
But my little knife is dull.
I can deny . . . and weep.
But, Lord,
I long for more.
Peter changed from human impetuosity
To heavenly power
So that walking on water,
Or using the sword was no longer important.
Instead, he preached and thousands found You.
He spoke and the lame man was healed.
People thronged for the magic of his shadow
To touch them.
This I may never do, Lord.
But whatever I do is important,
And can be done in the quiet power of
Thy Spirit.

So . . . help me, Lord,
        To be me . . . in Your power.

Lord,
She was seven today.
A magical age.
She won't even remember it
But I can never forget it.
Copper-haired.
Porcelain-skinned.
She never knew she put a lump in my throat
and a throb in my heart.
The high-up ponytail bobbled
As she danced with joy when she opened the presents.
She wanted a Bible.
A "real" one.
A "grown-up's" Bible . . . with gold edges.
Oh! how she squealed when she saw it.
Red with gold edges, and all her own.
Lord,
May it ever be an open book to her.
At seventy as well as seven.
She is just learning to read from its pages.
She struggled hard with the words,
And what joy as I feed them to her.
She is mine, Lord,
And I give her to You.
I could not give you any gift more precious to me
Than my seven-year-old
Auburn-haired
Imp-angel.
I am really giving her back to You
For she is Yours
By creation and purchase.
Take good care of her, Lord.

May she know the joy of having an imp-angel
With a seventh birthday.

So . . . help me, Lord,
    To care for this treasure entrusted to me.

Lord,
I watched them fleetingly in their childish glee
Running through the rain.
What wondrous joy they exulted.
They never knew I saw them
And their wet, soggy, stringing hair.
What exuberance.
It brought me to a start, Lord.
Where had the childish joy I first knew with You gone?
I saw in them the utter abandon and freedom
I first experienced in You
As Your newborn child.
I remembered the sheer radiance of a new day,
Just because I was Yours.
That was at first.
Then I became sophisticated . . . and lost the joy
Of my first love.
Lord,
How their radiance,
Viewed but for a fleeting moment
Pierced my soul,
Convicted me.
I need to come back, Lord.
I need to be a child again.
I want to be Your child again.

So . . . help me, Lord,
        To know the joy of my first love.

Lord,
I get so deadly serious,
So intently sure,
So blasted strait-laced.
I know You must laugh.
Not *at* me,
For You do not laugh at Your children,
But at the humor
Of my Little Lord Fauntleroy preciseness.
I need to be alert, yes,
But, Lord,
I also need to relax.
I need to learn to laugh at myself,
To take myself with a grain of salt.
All it takes, Lord,
Is to remember
That I will never come out of it alive.
Help me let go
And enjoy others as well as myself.
And the great fun of living.

So . . . help me, Lord,
        To remember I am just not THAT important.

Lord,
There are times my lips are inadequate
For the singing of my soul.
The joy wells up and overflows,
And words cannot convey my heart.
It is then the Spirit cries,
"Abba, Father."
And that is enough.
Thank You, Lord,
For the times of overflowing,
When not my lips
But my soul sings.
This should be normal
But it is usually abnormal,
And is often interspersed with dryness,
When no wells spring up from within,
And I walk,
Unfeeling,
But by faith,
Knowing that I could not be any earthly good
If all were the overflowing,
Without the dry seasons.
Thank You, Lord,
That the times of overflowing
Are not as necessary as they once were.
Maybe this is maturing,
Or trusting.

So . . . help me, Lord,
      That my soul may always sing.

Lord,
Not again! Surely not again.
We moved just a year ago.
That was the first time our girls could remember moving,
And now we have to do it again.
They were just getting settled in,
Now they don't want to leave.
The new house was just becoming "ours."
New friends, new schools, and a new church
Had just now begun to replace the old.
I know it will be hard on them, Lord,
To make another move so soon,
But thank You that children bounce back quickly.
They will adjust more rapidly than their parents
Who find tearing up roots more difficult with the passing of time.

The hardest part will be leaving our church.
It made our last move worth it all.
Our teen-ager will be brokenhearted, Lord.
This was her first year to be in the youth choir,
Take a choir tour, work in a telephone ministry,
And a hundred other things that teen-agers do in church.
I ask You to bless her especially.
Help her to know You order our every step . . . even a move.
Bless my wife, too, Lord.
Moving is hard on wives who must bear the brunt of the work.
(She owes me a move, Lord. She was in the hospital having a baby
    on one of our moves, and I always felt that was a sneaky way to
    get out of it.)
Keep us from begrudging having to move, Lord,
Remembering You never had a place to lay Your head.
And we do have that.

So . . . help me, Lord,
        When I would feel sorry for myself
        To recall You left Your Father's house . . . for me.

Lord,
I don't *really* want to escape.
There are times I feel like it.
I'm glad You don't let me.
For You know me,
Better than I know myself;
And You know
I would be pitifully remorseful
Before I got around the corner.
Besides that,
I'm just not the playboy type . . .
Even when I fancy myself so.
You know it just isn't true.
If anyone else knew,
They would laugh
That I even entertained the thought.
But what man hasn't entertained the thought?
Thank You, Lord,
That in this playboy world
The same standards make a man
As when You became a man.
It is the regular day-to-day meeting of life,
In all its routineness and sameness,
Its drabness and shabbiness,
Its sham and shame,
Without surrender
That makes a man.
I'm grateful You keep me from being a playboy.
Besides . . . I wouldn't know how.

So . . . help me, Lord,
        To remember that when the temptation comes.

Lord,
Forgive our sentimentality
That finds it easy to pray
In a pastoral setting,
But impossible
In the marketplace.
It is easy to pray when the lights are low,
When the organ swells,
Or the sun plays through the stained-glass windows.
But in the hard places,
The ugly places,
Where the people are also ugly,
Then, Lord,
Somehow even sentimentality does no good.
Oh, Lord,
We so compartmentalize You.
Forgive us . . .
Forgive *me* . . .
Teach me Your love
For that rough, crude, dirty urchin,
That rude customer,
That hard-nosed businessman.
And may I so let Your love flow unhindered
That I do not need the mountain retreat,
Or the cozy church,
Or the quietness of my special spot
To pray

So . . . help me, Lord,
　　　　To pray . . . and pray . . . and pray.

Lord,
There are times I feel like tiptoeing through life.
I know I should walk firmly,
Eagerly, courageously,
Willing to step in "where angels fear to tread."
I am just not that angelic.
It would be a lot easier to tiptoe,
Not ever rocking the boat,
Or taking a stand
Contrary to others,
Or the status quo.
But, Lord,
Don't let me.
You turned over the tables in the temple.
You drove out the money changers.
You were angered with the Pharisees,
The hypocrites,
The whited sepulchers.
You strode the hills of Galilee
With strength and purpose.
With gentility,
And kindness,
And tenderness.
But temerity . . . *never*.

So . . . help me, Lord,
  To walk firmly and gently, but not tiptoe.

Lord,
Yesterday's grace will not suffice for today's need.
I know I am not worthy
But I am needy.
And I come to You
To receive and accept the grace I need
For *this* day,
For *this* hour,
For *this* moment.
I do not even plan to endure this day.
I plan to live it fully and wholly.
In its afflictions and distresses,
In its tribulations and testings,
I reckon on Your grace as being sufficient.
Not yesterday, nor tomorrow, but *today*.
I draw upon Your grace *now*.
I could not know Your grace
Other than in my need.
So I thank You for making me needy,
Then being Yourself the supply of that need.
I do not deserve it.
If I did, it would not be grace—
I would merit it,
And I do not.

So . . . help me, Lord,
　　　To know *now* the sufficiency of Your grace.

Lord,
My wife is dieting again.
Bless her.
It's so hard on a wife to have a thin husband
When she is not.
She wasn't tiny when we married, Lord.
Seventeen years and two children later
Haven't helped the problem.
I loved every ounce of that beautiful pudgy girl, Lord,
And still do.
The worst part is that she gets down about it.
Our society equates a trim body with beauty.
Thank You, Lord, that this is not always so.
My wife belittles herself for her weight
And gets mad because of her lack of will power
To follow through on her diet plans.
Sooner or later the diets go by the board.
Lord, I could never even start a diet,
But she *does* start . . . and start . . . and start.
She can just smell water and gain weight.
I once thought anybody could be trim
But I don't feel that way any more.
I know the days ahead are going to tax her.
Help me and the girls to be patient, loving, and undemanding,
Especially about food.
Most of all, reassure her heart
That an extra pound here and there is not a tragedy.
Help her to know that her inner beauty, her love, her abilities and
    talents
Are the important things to me.

So . . . help me, Lord,
            To make sure she knows I feel this way,
            And not only when she is dieting.

Lord,
I thank You that You have invited me to come boldly to You.
I marvel that I can come at all—but boldly?
Most of the time I come timidly, Lord.
The things I long to say go unsaid,
For my tongue is dumb,
My mind is numb,
And I am wordless
From the pressures and burdens of life.
Thank You, Lord,
That at those times
Your Spirit speaks in my stead
And on my behalf,
For He knows my heart
And Your mind
And utters the deep things
I cannot speak.

Then, Lord, I more often say too much,
Too loudly,
Rather than in silence
Waiting and listening.
Forgive me for rushing irreverently
And noisily into Your presence
With my words instead of my heart.
My children do likewise, Lord.
So impetuously they speak,
Loudly saying little things.
And because they are mine,
I listen,
Just as You do with me.

So . . . help me, Lord,
To come to You
Again, and again, and again . . . and boldly.

Lord,
Forgive me for my "but what abouts?"
You ask of me,
And I can only reply
"But what about . . . ?"
As if to imply that Your demands
Are greater than Your empowering.
Father, help me to know
That my limitation of natural ability
Has no place in the things of the Spirit.
When I ask "but what about . . . ?"
I am only looking to my natural ability
To accomplish, to perform,
While You are simply wanting
The power of Your Spirit to do
What I cannot,
To fill up that
Which I lack.

So . . . help me, Lord,
    Not to confuse my ability
    With Your enabling.

Lord,
Thank You for the beautiful, uninhibited love of children.
They love so easily and freely.
Like my daughter number two.

I had been gone for the weekend.
A snow and ice storm hit suddenly
Catching me in its blinding cold fury as I drove home.
It was a dangerous drive, taking several hours longer than usual.
I was completely drained physically from the tenseness of the drive
    on ice.
The family was awaiting me anxiously
And greeted me joyously with hugs and kisses.
But the nine year old met me with a large, hand-lettered sign that
    said
"T. G. P. H."
Which, being interpreted, means
"Thank God, Papa's home."

Men can't cry in front of their children, Lord,
They just get lumps in their throats
And quickened heartbeats.
There are times they would rather cry.

So . . . help me, Lord.
        To be such a father that she will always say
        "T. G. P. H."

45

Lord,
You said "render unto Caesar,"
But, good grief,
Why does Caesar need so much?
I'm working more for Caesar
Than for me.
I'm glad to pay him his due,
But, somehow, I don't believe he is due *that* much.
Like a greedy child he keeps saying
"More, more, more."
And the untold hours I have to spend in my business
Just proving to Caesar
That he *is* getting his due.
I feel like charging him for my time,
But I know he would never pay.
And, Lord,
I resent his making me feel guilty
Even when I give him his due.

Lord, forgive me.
It's just tax time again.
I really am grateful
For the privilege of paying tribute—
Even to Caesar.
And he is due a great deal.
He has given me America,
Freedom, and relatively little invasion of my life.
May it always be the land of the free,
The home of the brave,
And the place where "in God we trust"
Is more than a motto.

So . . . help me, Lord,
    To render unto Caesar joyfully.

Lord,
Must I always weigh the pros and cons?
It is always right to obey.
That is what I want in my children.
Implicit and instant obedience.
But with You, Lord,
How often I weigh the consequences,
And make the awesome mistake
Of disobedience.
Sometimes I think I do so
Because I may not understand,
And feel mistaken in discerning what You have said,
Thus fearing I will dishonor You.
In doing so I become more loyal
To my ideas of the way You work
Than to You.
So I try to clear the way
With reasoning,
Intelligence,
Logic,
Rather than faithful obedience.
Teach me, Lord,
The joy of reckless abandon and instant obedience.

So . . . help me, Lord,
     To remember that "to obey is better than
       to sacrifice."

Lord,
The marketplace is so everyday.
So menial.
And so dog-eat-dog
That it is difficult to find You there.
I have to look—hard.
It is easy to find You in church,
Or in the place of prayer,
But in the marketplace?
When others are being unjust
Surely You do not expect me to be just,
And honest, and give full measure
In the marketplace?
Who cares there?
There it's just money, money, money.
Then I remember.
You, Lord,
Were more often with the sinner
Than saint.
You were among the people,
In the busy hustle and bustle.
You were fair and honest,
And robust and manly
And uncompromising.
How great it is, Lord,
That even in the marketplace
You remind me I am Yours.
In the hectic, cruel maelstrom of business
You nudge me,
Or whisper to me,
Or give me a good strong poke
To let me know that you expect the same of me
In the marketplace

As in the church place.
That businessman is lonely . . .
That secretary is scared . . .
That lawyer is tired . . .
They are all unknowingly looking for You,
And I may be the only glimpse they will ever see
Of Your life . . . Your love.

So . . . help me, Lord,
    In the marketplace.

Lord,
Forgive me for being anxious about material things.
I *do* want to give my family the best,
And surely that is right.
It's a man's responsibility to provide
For his loved ones.
But I get in kinks and knots . . .
And worry and fear
Lest I should not be able to do it.
This is wrong, Lord.
I know You want me to work hard . . .
This I like,
For You knew man needed work,
But You want me to trust harder than I work,
And depend on You,
Remembering that You clothe the lilies of the field,
You provide for the fowls of the air,
And You said I am much more to you than they.
Their glory exceeds that of Solomon's,
And not one sparrow falls to the ground
Without the Father.

But I sometimes forget to seek You first,
And Your kingdom.
I forget that all these things will be added,
So I worry and fret.
Will I ever learn that Your love
Is free . . . and full . . . and includes the material
As well as the spiritual?

So . . . help me, Lord,
     To look to You to provide.

Lord,
I call it humility.
"I am not worthy . . .
  I am incapable . . .
  Not *me,* Lord . . ."
Lord, You know better.
You know it is not humility . . .
It is self-reliance.
If I were You, I think I would be sick of me.
It sounds so humble and pious, Lord,
But in reality it is just plain self-centeredness,
Or laziness.
Of course You want me to be humble.
Of course You do not want me to think more highly of myself
Than I should.
But neither do You want me to use that as an excuse
To justify my not following or obeying You.
Why *not* me?
Poor little old me . . .
Even if I am unworthy (and I am)
So is everybody else.
None of us is worthy to be called of You.
But You are able to enable me, Lord.
So my humility,
My seeking to escape a commitment,
Or a task from You,
Is not humility.
It is disobedience.
For Your callings are Your enablings.

So . . . help me, Lord,
        To discern between humility and disobedience.

Lord,
I have been thinking about Job today.
Could he have been a mortal like me?
The man stuns me.
He leaves me dumb, and numb.
Not because of his patience,
So much as his faithfulness in affliction.
For what man could say,
"Though God slay me, yet will I trust Him,"
When he had experienced the trials of Job?
Or who could say,
"When He has tried me I shall come forth as gold?"
For me, Lord,
It would have been sheer effrontery,
But for Job it was true.
Job was true to his word.

I know he was mortal
For he longed for the days gone by,
And those to come.
Which shows me he endured,
But did not enjoy
The hard places.
That would have made him more than mortal.
I would have the patience of Job.
I know this means tribulation,
For Your Word says, "Tribulation worketh patience."
I wish there were another way,
But there is not.

So . . . help me, Lord,
       To endure as Job, and come forth as gold.

Lord,
My heart leaped with joy
As they ran to greet me.
It was a hard trip
And I had been gone so long,
And I had missed them so.
They were my children,
And as they ran to meet me,
I wondered if they had missed me, too.
I remember thinking they must be thrilled
To see their father.
But they only asked,
"What did you bring us, Papa?"
It hurt my ego too
Until I remembered . . .
How like me,
When I come to You, Lord.
Often I am more interested in Your gifts
Than in You.

I am grateful You understand,
Just as I understood . . .
And gave them their gifts.
I knew they loved me more than the gifts
Because I was their father.
How good to know You know
I really do love You more than Your gifts,
Even when I don't act like it
And like a spoiled child
Am forever asking . . . asking . . . asking.

So . . . help me, Lord,
      To praise more and ask less.

Lord,
You must have been grieved today
At my expressed surprise
When You answered prayer.
As though it were a miracle,
Or unexpected.

It should be no surprise that You answer prayer.
It should be expected . . .
And every day.
Forgive us that we forget
The "how much more" of our Heavenly Father.

I would be saddened if my children
Asked of me,
Only to express surprise
When I granted their requests.
"How much more" do You want to grant ours.
The surprise is that we don't ask more.
We have not because we ask not.
I do not give my children a stone
When they want candy.
Nor do I give them poison
When they are thirsty.
I give freely,
Joyfully,
Because I am able
And they depend on me.
"How much more" our Heavenly Father.

So . . . help me, Lord,
        To depend on you . . . and to ask . . . believing.

Lord,
It must be awfully hard to be ten
When your sister is fourteen,
And getting a ten-speed bicycle
Or a new guitar,
And taking a choir-tour to Guatemala.
It's true, we've told her
These things would come to her, too,
When she is fourteen, and can
Handle them.
But a ten-year-old heart hurts, too.
I pray, Lord, that she will know
It is a difference in age,
Not a difference in love
That brings these benefits to her
Older sister.
I'll take her to see a movie tonight, Lord.
Just her and me.
And I'll buy her popcorn,
And hold her hand,
And love her till my heart hurts.
I guess the benefits of age are always
Harder
When you are the younger.

So . . . help me, Lord,
      To make sure she reaps the benefits
        When she is fourteen.

Lord,
I have tasted and found Thee good.
I was so hungry.
Now the deep, gnawing pain of emptiness
Has vanished.
And I am satisfied.
Now I need to feed on Thee,
Bread of life.
Help me to taste fully,
And deeply
Of Thee.
That in tasting, my satisfaction
May make others hunger
After Thee.
I have found Thee good.
I have found Thee love.
I have found Thee
To be all my hungering and thirsting soul
Had craved.

So . . . help me, Lord,
        And "Feed me till I want no more."

Lord,
I work so hard at being a Christian.
Just like that big jet straining for the sky,
Pulling so powerfully
Seeking floating freedom.

So like me, Lord.
I always seem to be pulling.
At times I glide gracefully,
And imagine I have reached a safe height
Where I can coast effortlessly,
Only to plummet earthward,
Pulled relentlessly
By the law of human gravity—sin.
I yearn to soar,
To scale the heights
And there be free of this world's tug.
But that is not to be in this life,
Except for eagles, or birds, or satellites.
One day, though, it will be different, Lord.
For I shall mount up with wings as eagles.
I shall put off this mortal
To be clothed with immortality,
Free . . . soaring.
Till then, Lord,
Help me remember that this world's pull
Is to remind me of my dependence on You.

So . . . help me, Lord,
      To walk uprightly till then.

Lord,
The sound was so strange.
Especially with my wife still lying in bed beside me.
It was the sound of dishes and silverware.
The sound of a table being set.
Then I looked in her room.
The bed was made.
All her stuffed animals and dolls
Were lined neatly in their places,
And I knew immediately it was my ten-year-old
In the kitchen.
When I went in she was so busy,
Singing as she worked.
It was Sunday morning and
She was preparing breakfast.

My heart leaped to my throat
As I watched the beauty of a happy child.
"Good morning, Papa," she chirped.
I wondered why the sudden beehive of activity,
The open faced happiness.
Until I remembered.
I had taken her to a movie the night before.
It was wonderful—just the two of us.
The movie was so exciting she trembled.
I gave her my coat,
And held her hand,
And explained all the parts she did not comprehend.
We laughed, and loved the whole two hours.
Lord, thank You,
For what a little attention can do for a child.

So . . . help me, Lord,
    To never get too busy
        To make memories for my children.

Lord,
It seemed foolish and expensive
To spend so much time, money, and effort
To be together for the weekend.
She had to fly two thousand miles.
Arrangements had to be made for someone to take care of the girls.
We had to lease a car, get motel rooms, find places to eat.
It really was a lot of trouble
Just for a husband and wife, married seventeen years,
To share a weekend.
Thank You, Lord, that we went to the trouble.

Thank You, Lord, for the mystical union of a man and woman.
Even a mystical union, however,
Needs the cultivation only time alone together can give.
It's not that we don't love our children, our home.
But being together, sharing our silly moments,
Our physical moments,
Brings a new glow and warmth
So often paled as the years go by.

It was worth it, Lord.
Now she is leaving for home,
And I must stay here on business another week.
It will be a longer week than if she had not come,
For now I will miss her more.

So . . . help us, Lord,
        To be willing to go to all the trouble necessary
        To keep marriage a glowing, joyous union.

Lord,
I can get the words out,
But the heart belief is something else.
I want to be able to say with the writer of scripture
"Do that which seemeth good to Thee."
But when I do
Things get all fouled up.
Instead of all going well
Trials and testings come.
Hard places come,
Tribulations and darkness come.
On every side
I see those who shine
In the limelighted, glamorous side of Christianity.
Nothing seems to go wrong.
They have it made,
Financially and emotionally,
Socially and spiritually.
But in me there is always the churning
Of doubt, fear, and frustration.
Am I so doubting?
Am I so far from You, Lord,
That You cannot send me
The fame, the glamour, the finances,
The poise You send others?
Thank You, Lord, for Job.
Surely this was what he felt
As he struggled through his
Dark night of the soul.
Lord, I want to come forth as he did.
And be able to say,

"Though God slay me,
Yet will I trust Him."

It seems, for me, at least,
That the path of testings and trials
Is the only way this can be.

So . . . help me, Lord,
        And do what seems good to Thee.

Lord,
"Pray through" I hear them say.
All my life I've heard "pray through,"
As if there were a barrier
Beyond which,
If I could break it,
I would find praying easy,
Spontaneous,
Miraculous,
Answered.
So I have labored to "pray through,"
Whatever that meant.
But prayer never ceased to be labor,
Or a struggle
Which required effort and energy.
Nor have there been miracles,
Or instant answers.
There *has* been fellowship,
Communion, love, devotion,
And joy,
So that the effort has had its reward.
But Lord,
I think I now know what they mean
When they say "pray through."
Isn't it just praying
Till you come to the "putting down place,"
The place where burdens are "put down"?
Trials are "put down,"
Sorrow is "put down,"
And the innumerable things that press us,
So that daily—no—moment by moment we
"Put down" at your feet
That which causes us to be heavy laden.

So . . . help me, Lord,
          To pray to the "putting down" place.

Lord,
I pray today that You will help me
Be the father to my children You are to me;
So that in time, the trust they have given me
May be transferred to You.
Oh, that I might be
Their rock,
Their tower,
Their strength,
Their shield,
Their comfort.
For these You are to me.
Father,
You have taught me much about Yourself
Through my children.
I love them when they are good,
I think I almost love them more when they are bad . . .
For then their need is greater,
Just as I need You . . .
Just as I have You . . .
May I be faithful, in love,
To discipline them as You discipline me.
If I ever need proof that I am Yours,
I have it when You discipline me,
For I do not discipline my neighbor's children . . .
Only my own. And so do You.
Grant me the joy of showing them You.
For if I do all else,
And fail to point them to the Heavenly Father,
I have failed as an earthly father.

So . . . help me, Lord,
        As a Father.

Lord,
I hear it on every hand.
"Faith is all right, but in business
You've got to use common sense."
I know that sounds good, Lord,
But is faith the opposite of common sense?
Good common sense is necessary in business,
But there are times when it runs crosswise to faith.
It didn't make sense for Abraham to strike out,
"Not knowing whither he went."
But Abraham believed God,
And, Lord, You counted it to Him for righteousness.
There were times, Lord,
When "good common sense" would have robbed me
Of the joy of seeing You supply my needs.
Like the customer we needed,
Or the one we didn't get,
Yet still believed You would meet our needs,
And You did.
I know that faith does not make me immune
To diligence,
Faithfulness,
And plain old hard work.
Nor do I want to be presumptuous, Lord,
But I do believe that even a businessman
Can trust You with his business,
And recklessly count on Your faithfulness,
And can trust You to give wisdom and guidance.

So . . . help me, Lord,
        To trust You in my business.

Lord,
Happiness is knowing You.
I simply bow today to thank You
For the joy and happiness that have been mine
Since You found me.
Lord, I am happier now
When I am unhappy
Than I was before
When I was happy.
Oh, not in a bubbly, bouncy way,
But a deep settled peace,
An awareness of You,
And a knowledge that I am Yours.
Thank You, Lord,
For the fountain of life,
For the rivers of living water
That flow from the recesses of my soul
And fill me with Your love, joy, and peace.
Even if there were no immortal life,
What You have brought to this mortal one
Makes it all worth while.

So . . . help me, Lord,
    That Your living water may flow from me to others.

Lord,
I thank You for the mountains.
They respond so warmly to my love.
Hardly a day in the marketplace goes by
That I do not long for my mountains.
You are not there
More so than anywhere else,
But You seem to be nearer there.
I do not think it strange
That You retired to a mountain to pray.
And You gave the law to Moses on a mountain.
There you fed the five thousand
And there Abraham offered Isaac.
On top of a mountain Elijah did away
With four hundred prophets of Baal,
And the ark rested atop a mountain.
On the mount You were transfigured . . . and crucified.
It is no wonder to me that the Psalmist
Looked unto the hills.
My heart goes there often, Lord.
But I rejoice that I do not have to wait
To be in the mountains
To have a mountain-top experience with You.

So . . . help me, Lord,
    To reach new heights with You each day.

Lord,
I have not forgotten all those dreams.
Nor have I given up those noble ambitions.
But, somehow, Lord,
The years have changed me.
I no longer need nobility
As much as discipline.
Discipline should have been my path,
But dreaming was easier.
Now I know, I trust not too late,
That nobility can never come
To the undisciplined.
"Shaping up" did not seem so important then.
Maybe it is just that there is less time now,
And it seems more important that I be something
Than that I *do* something.
Doing something is fairly easy,
But being something—Lord,
That seems impossible.

So . . . help me, Lord,
        To forfeit dreams for discipline.

Lord,
We're just taking off again.
The plane seems to be going straight up,
Straining against gravity to touch the upper reaches of the sky.
I have that empty feeling inside.
The feeling of aloneness, of emptiness.
It happens everytime I have to leave home,
Which seems to be increasingly more.
Maybe some guys like to leave home
For the freedom a time away provides,
But not me, Lord.
The ache will be deep inside me till I return.
It never seems to get easier.
There is always the gnawing yearning to be home.
I trust, Lord,
It is not just a desire to be in familiar surroundings
Which does offer comfort,
But the desire to be with those I love . . . my wife, my girls, my dog.
Is it like this with others, Lord,
Or am I the only one who feels his love more when he is away from
    the family?
I miss my wife already,
And were I with her at this moment
I would tell her so.
I would let her know I am grateful
For the great job she does being both mother and father
While I am away.
Bless her, Lord,
And if she feels the same emptiness I feel,
Comfort her and assure her of my love.
Bless the girls,

For even though they appear nonchalant
I know they get uptight when I'm gone.

So . . . help me, Lord,
To show when I am with them
What I feel when I have to leave them.

Lord,
The die is cast.
I'm stuck.
There's no way out.
The point of no return
Was passed long ago,
And like Peter, I have to say
"To whom shall we go, Lord . . . ?"
True, I now and then look, and long,
For the leeks and garlic of Egypt,
With a pull in that direction.
But I could never go back, Lord.
I don't really want to,
Except in those moments.
The man inside knows we could never go back.
Lord, forgive those times
Of murmuring,
Of complaining
About the hardness of the way.
Help me remember the way of the transgressor
Is much harder.
Thank you, Lord,
That You have placed inside me
That longing after Yourself
That negates the pull of the old man
And causes my heart to yearn after Thee.
No turning back now, Lord.
It's too late for that.

So . . . help me, Lord,
       To set my face toward Thee
       Without a care for the world's pull.

Lord,
I'm sick and tired of "re" preachers.
They tell me I need to
"Re-dedicate" or
"Re-consecrate," etc., *ad nauseam.*
It sounds like they want me to be
Just a "re-tread."
Thank You, Lord,
That You don't make me "re" anything.
I am Yours.
It is as simple as that.
You created me,
Purchased me,
Sealed me,
And are coming for me.
So, there's nothing more to be done.
I don't have to "re-do" me, Lord.
You took me, just as I was.
No need for me to "re-affirm"
That I won't "re-peat" that sin . . .
We both know better.
Likely, that will be the next thing I do.
And . . . if it is . . .
Neither You nor I "re-do" a thing.
I simply confess,
And I am "re-stored" to fellowship.

So . . . help me, Lord,
      To "re-flect" You.

Lord,
Thank You for my beautiful teen-aged daughter.
I've loved her so,
Even from right after the moment of birth
When they placed her in my arms,
And she was so porcelain white.
I was so relieved,
For I just knew she would be red-faced
And crying.

She has become such a mature young lady.
Tenderhearted, unselfish, talented,
With an infectious sense of humor.
The quality about her that moves me most, Lord,
Is her deep love for You.
In her love for You, she loves others.
She is obedient without being servile.
She is joyous without being pious.
She is lovely inwardly
And beautiful outwardly.
How I do thank You, Lord.
I don't deserve a daughter like this.
Other fathers seem so bewildered
By their offspring.
So many have turned against their parents.
I hear of so much enmity between
Parent and child.
I marvel this is not so with us.
We have no barrier, no gap.
How blessed I am, Lord,
And I bow before You
With a joyous, grateful heart
For this lovely teen-aged daughter.

So . . . help me, Lord,
        To be as good a father
            As she is a daughter.

Lord,
It's today that counts.
I idly dream of tomorrow,
Or relive yesterday's memories,
And forget today.
Today is all that I have, Lord.
Tomorrow will be wonderful,
Yesterday was unforgettable,
But I will never have today again.
Today's blue sky is just for today.
The day lily is just today's alone,
Tomorrow its bloom is gone,
Never to return.
This intimacy I share with You, Lord,
Is just today's.
I want to be aware of today's smell of bacon,
Of today's tear,
Or lilting laughter,
For that laughter will be lost in the wind
And that tear dried on the cheek before tomorrow.
And it is today only
That You can live in me.

So . . . help me, Lord,
        To *live* today.

Lord,
I need to be a little boy again for a while.
I don't think You mind.
It may be immature,
But not wrong.
Doesn't everybody need to be a child again at times?
I know that in these times
I can turn to You as a child,
Even as I turned to my earthly father,
When I really was a child,
And You will tend my hurts,
Calm my fears,
Soothe and smooth things over,
And send me on my way.
Thank You, Lord,
That You don't get mad at me
For wanting to be a little boy again . . .
Even when I act like one.
Does Your Father heart smile
At my childishness?
When I pout, or cry,
Or throw a tantrum?
Or when I am very, very good,
Or try to act so grown-up
And blunder so badly,
Trying to be so strong and manly,
When You know that inside I am putty and weak,
And scared—like a child?
Maybe You smile,
But thank You,
That You do not laugh.

So . . . help me, Lord,
        To be childlike but not childish.

Lord,
Thank You that I do not have a golden halo.
I rarely know the flush of inspiration.
Seldom do I have moments of spiritual ecstasy.
It is not that You have not touched me,
Nor spoken,
Nor melted me.
But that was when You knew
That in my infancy I needed it.
Now you expect better things,
Like walking by faith
When the heavens seem shut,
When the rivers seem dry.
Lord, keep me from making a fetish
Of the rare,
The intimate moments,
Or seeking a "new touch,"
Or insisting that You do anything again.
This only proves I do not want You,
But what You give.
Keep me from desiring the illuminated spot,
Where saints seek me.
Teach me to walk moment by moment
Doing that which is at hand,
Expecting nothing in return.
Then I can enjoy the surprises
Of those moments when You come . . .
In the stillness of the night,
Or in the midst of the throng.

So . . . help me, Lord,
      To seek only You . . . not Your gifts.

Lord,
I thought the preacher
Had more faith than anybody else.
But that's all wrong.
Lord, it takes a lot more gutsy faith
To be a businessman than a preacher.
His salary is paid . . . rather well, too.
And he is worthy of his hire.
No complaints there.
But the preacher cannot know
The blind faith it takes
To trust You in the dog-eat-dog world
Of the marketplace.
To trust You, Lord, enough to be scrupulous
In an unscrupulous world.
Or honest in a dishonest age.
But more than that,
It takes faith to trust You
For every customer,
And to be concerned for every customer
That he gets what he needs,
Even if it means a smaller sale.
And then to give him what he *really* needs,
A testimony of Your love for him.
And Lord, it is not a gamble.
It is a sure thing
When by faith I entrust, not only myself,
But my business to You.
For some, taking You as their business partner
Has meant fantastic financial prosperity,
But not so with me, Lord.
There has just been enough.
But oh, how my faith has grown.

So . . . help me, Lord,
        To be busy trusting You.

Lord,
It always surprises me
That when I see myself,
I also see You.
No one but You could see me as I am,
And take me as I am.
I know You try to change me . . .
Not because You dislike the way I am,
But because what You want me to become
Is so much better.
When I realize this, Lord,
I quit chafing,
Sit back and enjoy watching You change me.
Like today . . .
The sight of him always piques me.
It leaves me uncomfortable . . . and pharisaical.
Smugness always feels so good—at first.
It was different today.
I asked You to make me be hard on myself
And gentle toward others.
So, when I saw him today, I felt differently.
I felt compassion.
I saw he was a man like me,
Inconsistent, brash, intolerant.
But today it did not matter.
I saw that he was also needy,
Fearful, and lonely.
And You reached out to him through me.

So . . . help me, Lord,
        To be gentle toward others and hard on myself.

Lord,
When I became a man
I put away childish things.
Or so I thought.
This morning I was awfully childish.
I wanted my way.
Just as when we used to "play like"
And I always had to be the big man.
I did it again, Lord.
I had to be the big man.
It turns out I was nothing but a spoiled child,
Scheming and pouting to get my own way
In a household where I am supposed to be the head.
But Lord, they wouldn't let me be the head.
So I became a child again,
And acted like one.
Will I ever learn
That if I am to be the man of the house
I must be one in every area?
Being an adult doesn't make me a man.
I thought I was entitled to have my way
Because I was the head of the house . . . the big man.
And I only proved again that I was a child.

So . . . help me, Lord,
            To humble myself as a child
            That I may be a man.

Lord,
In this hectic hippie world
Of psychedelic colors,
Of screaming music
I would be hopelessly pessimistic
Without the deep assurance
That You are still on Your throne
And still in control.
At times it seems our universe is Godforsaken.
Not that I could blame You, Lord.
But this is not You . . . to leave us alone.
Or forsake us in the face of ourselves.
They hold up two fingers in the peace symbol.
They speak of love
While destroying all love and beauty.
It would drive me mad, Lord,
But I remember the song.
"Jesus, Lover of my soul
Let me to Thy bosom fly,
While the nearer waters roll,
While the tempest still is high."
"Other refuge have I none,
Hangs my helpless soul on Thee . . ."
Thank You, Lord,
For the great cries of the human heart
That have hung themselves on words
And become our great hymns.

So . . . help me, Lord,
To remember that "plenteous grace with Thee is found."

Lord,
I want to be head of my house,
Especially in things spiritual.
It is a lot easier to let my wife
Handle this area.
It surely must be all right
In this feminine liberated age.
But Lord,
My children need to hear *me* read Your Word,
They need to see *me* on my knees in prayer.
It is Your plan for it to be so.
I am unable to provide them with wealth,
But I can show them my dependence on You.
I can lead them in the faith.
I can give them the only lasting heritage.
But it is difficult, Lord.
So many business demands.
Social demands.
Demands on my time,
Until, if I am not careful,
The day is done
And everyone is scattered and tired,
And I have wasted another opportunity
To lead my family in the things of the Lord.
Lord, I pray for diligence,
Strength and courage
To lead spiritually in my home.
It is not my wife's job,
It is mine.

So . . . help me, Lord,
        To lead them as You lead me.

Lord,
I often marvel
That You let me be a father and husband.
As a husband I am not much.
I am not big and brawny.
I'm not even brainy.
I don't make a lot of money.
The comforts I am able to secure
Are modest compared to many men.
I'm not good with my hands.
I can't fix faucets,
Or add on a room,
Or do those many manly things around a house.
I'm a lousy lover,
But I do love her.
As a father I don't rate too highly either.
The toys go unmended.
I'm not good at roughhousing,
Or fishing, or hunting,
Or those "big" things that rate a father tall.
But I do have one redeeming factor
For which I thank You, Lord.
And that is that I love.
I love being a husband.
I love being tender to my wife.
I love the life we share, and
Especially as we share it with You.
And I love my children.
I love to love them,
And have them love me.
I love being gentle and kind to them.
I love to supply their needs,
And tend their wounds,

Both physical and otherwise.
My only qualification for being a husband and father
Is my love for them.

So . . . help me, Lord,
To be the best one possible.

Lord,
Choices are always in my path.
Thank You.
How loving You are
To let me choose
Whether I choose to love You,
Or hate.
How loathesome is forced love.
Only the choice
Can give love its meaning.
So, Lord,
I choose to love You,
For You are my God.
There are other gods I could choose,
But they are enslaving,
Binding,
And give me no choice but slavery.
They do not return my love.
They give hate and death instead.
I choose You, Lord,
In preference . . .
Just as I chose my wife
In preference to all others
I could have chosen.
I did so in love.
I do so now with You,
Because choice gives life to love.

So . . . help me, Lord,
          To choose You always.

Lord,
It hit me hard today.
It was our anniversary . . . and
It suddenly dawned on me.
She chose me.
She gave her life to me.
She could have had her pick,
And she picked me.
She might have married a wise man,
Or a rich man,
Or a strong man . . .
But she married me.
It awes me to know
She gave her life to me.
She follows me, soothes my nerves,
Cooks my meals, irons my clothes,
Loves me when I'm good,
And . . . I think . . . when I'm bad.
She bore my children, and sometimes
Babies me more than them.
I thank You, Lord, for her.
Somehow, make up to her, Lord,
For all she missed
By choosing me.

So . . . help me, Lord,
        To be a good husband.

Lord,
Must it always be guitars?
There must not be a teen-ager in the land
Who does not feel that a guitar is a
Ticket to heaven.
Most I hear are played badly
Or too loudly.
My ears would much prefer David's
Melodious harp,
Or the velvet beauty of a violin or cello.
I suppose that because guitars are so numerous
They seem common.
But not to the youth—and not to my
Violinist, pianist, teen-ager.

I held out a long time.
Long enough to make her want it all the more.
But it became a passion, a craving, a hunger
That could be fulfilled by one thing only—
A guitar.
So yesterday, we bought a guitar.
We haven't seen her since.
She lives in her room—playing, playing, playing.
Playing badly, but playing.
And I'm sure it was a ticket to her heaven.
And she is completely enthralled,
Engulfed in a world of six strings,
And sore fingers that are unaccustomed to
The feel of steel.
What a small price to pay for giving her joy.
Thank You, Lord,
For the joy of giving joy to my children.
I pray You will keep her
From letting that guitar be a ticket to the hell

Of drugs, rock festivals,
And all that has made adults afraid of guitars.

I just remembered, Lord,
I played the guitar for years—and rather well, too.
It passed, along with other youthful delights,
And now I can't play even one simple chord.
It didn't hurt me.

So . . . help me, Lord,
   To always be sensitive to the tickets
   To happiness
    A father can give his children.

Lord,
It's a good thing I don't have to "feel" saintly.
More times than not I feel far less.
In fact, were the truth known
(And it is to *You*)
I usually feel far more (d)evilish than saintly.
It should not be any comfort
That I am in a vast majority,
But it is—which proves my point.
Saints have such a disadvantage.
They live in glass houses.
With You, I don't have to do that,
For I am already revealed to You.
You *know* me.
The inside me.
The me nobody has seen.
Because You know me
I don't have to put on
For You take me . . . just as I am . . .
No strings attached,
Understanding my unsaintliness,
Loving me anyway.
If I were saintly
I could expect Your love.
This way it is a surprise.

So . . . help me, Lord,
          In my unsaintliness.

Lord,
What is the matter with me?
Everybody knows men are supposed to be hard as nails.
But me . . . I'm just a sentimental pushover.
Like this morning.
That little copper-haired imp-angel
Cheerily chirped, "Have a good day, Papa,"
And skipped off to school.
The joy of it was painful.
I don't know that I like
Having to choke back the tears.
Lord,
I even have to fight the lump in my throat
When they play the school song,
Or "The Star-Spangled Banner"
At a football game.
I sometimes feel a sense of sheer ecstasy
When my wife or children tell me they love me.
Aren't men supposed to be tough?
Well, I'm not "so tough, but oh so gentle."
I'm just a softie.
My heart wells within me
At the beauty of the earth,
The song of the mockingbird,
Or the aspen in autumn.
Thank You, Father,
That my heart is not hard.

So . . . help me, Lord,
    To always be a softie.

Lord,
It has been a wonderful day.
The slow rain fell all night.
Today we have been ice-bound,
Loving every minute of it.
The TV has hardly been on.
We have ooohed and aaahed at the beauty of the ice
As it has thickened on the streets, on the trees.
We have watched the kids ice skating down the alley,
Some gracefully and some not.
We have played together and lazed together
While the fireplace has roared, friendly and warm.
Thank You, Lord,
For the beauty of an ice storm and a fireplace in full flame.

The most fun, though, was making bread.
Daughter number two and I
Spent hours making two big loaves of brown bread.
Boy, were we amateur bakers!
But the bread tasted good.
We wouldn't have cared if it hadn't,
For the smell of it baking, and the joy of making it
Were wages enough.

I really think, Lord,
You ought to give us at least one ice- or snow-bound day a year.
There was no rush, no plan, no care.
We talked, ate, played, laughed, and loved.

So . . . help me, Lord,
To learn to live each day as fully and joyously
As this ice-bound glorious day.